CLIMATE CHANGE
iN THE ARCTiC

STUART BAKER

Marshall Cavendish
Benchmark

New York

This edition first published in 2010 in the United States of America
by Marshall Cavendish Benchmark.

Marshall Cavendish Benchmark
99 White Plains Road
Tarrytown, NY 10591
www.marshallcavendish.us

First published in 2009 by
MACMILLAN EDUCATION AUSTRALIA PTY LTD
15–19 Claremont Street, South Yarra 3141

Visit our website at www.macmillan.com.au or go directly to www.macmillanlibrary.com.au

Associated companies and representatives throughout the world.

Library of Congress Cataloging-in-Publication Data

Baker, Stuart.
   In the Arctic / by Stuart Baker.
      p. cm. – (Climate change)
   ISBN 978-0-7614-4437-4
   1. Arctic peoples–Juvenile literature. 2. Human ecology–Arctic
   regions–Juvenile literature. 3. Arctic regions–Juvenile literature. I.
   Title.
   GN673.B37 2010
   971.9–dc22
                                    2009005767

Edited by Sally Woollett
Text and cover design by Christine Deering
Page layout by Christine Deering
Illustrations by Richard Morden
Photo research by Legend Images

Printed in the United States

Acknowledgments
The author and the publisher are grateful to the following for permission to reproduce
copyright material:

Front cover photograph: Inuit elder hunting on Baffin Island, Nunavut, Canada, courtesy of
Henry Georgi/Getty Images
Photos courtesy of:
© Danita Delimont/Alamy, **26**; ARCUS, photo by Sarah Behr, **10**; ARCUS, photo by Birte Horn-
Hanssen, **16**; Ira Block/Getty Images, **23**; Henry Georgi/Getty Images, **30**; George F. Mobley/
National Geographic/Getty Images, **27**; Richard Olsenius/Getty Images, **25**; Uriel Sinai/Getty
Images, **20**, **21**; © Meppu/iStockphoto, **14**; NASA, **8**, **9**; NASA Earth Observatory, **5**; NASA
images created by Jesse Allen, Earth Observatory, using data obtained from the University
of Maryland's Global Land Cover Facility, **17**; NASA image created by Jesse Allen, using
data obtained from the Goddard Land Processes data archives (LAADS), **24**; Photolibrary ©
Bryan & Cherry Alexander Photography/Alamy, **15**; Photolibrary © Ashley Cooper/Alamy, **22**;
Photolibrary © Leslie Garland Picture Library/Alamy, **29** (top); Photolibrary/Steven Kazlowski,
13; Photolibrary/Photo Researchers, **12**; Photolibrary/Bjorn Svensson/SPL, **19**; Provided by
the SeaWiFS Project, NASA/Goddard Space Flight Center, and ORBIMAGE, **18**; UN Photo/Evan
Schneider, **29** (bottom).

While every care has been taken to trace and acknowledge copyright, the publisher tenders
their apologies for any accidental infringement where copyright has proved untraceable.
Where the attempt has been unsuccessful, the publisher welcomes information that would
redress the situation.

1 3 5 6 4 2

Contents

Glossary Words	When a word is printed in **bold**, you can look up its meaning in the Glossary on page 31.

Climate Change

Earth has been warming and cooling for millions of years. During the **Ice Age**, large areas of Europe and Canada were covered with **glaciers**. Earth's climate was 5.4–9°Fahrenheit (3–5°Celsius) cooler than it is today. The most recent Ice Age ended 20,000 years ago.

Rising Temperatures

Temperatures across the world are rising at a rate faster than ever before. Earth's average temperature has risen by 1.08°F (0.6°C) in the past one hundred years. The ten hottest years on record occurred over the past fourteen years. The hottest year ever recorded was 2005. This **global warming** may be enough to cause changes in weather patterns, which is commonly referred to as **climate change**.

Earth's Climate Zones

Earth can be divided into four main types of climate zones:

- Arctic

- Temperate

- Tropical

- Antarctic

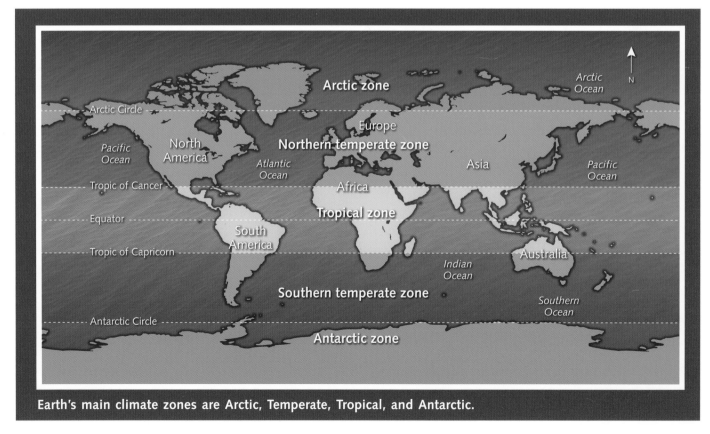

Earth's main climate zones are Arctic, Temperate, Tropical, and Antarctic.

The Arctic Region

The Arctic consists of the North Pole and the land and sea north of the Arctic Circle. It includes the Arctic Ocean and parts of several countries.

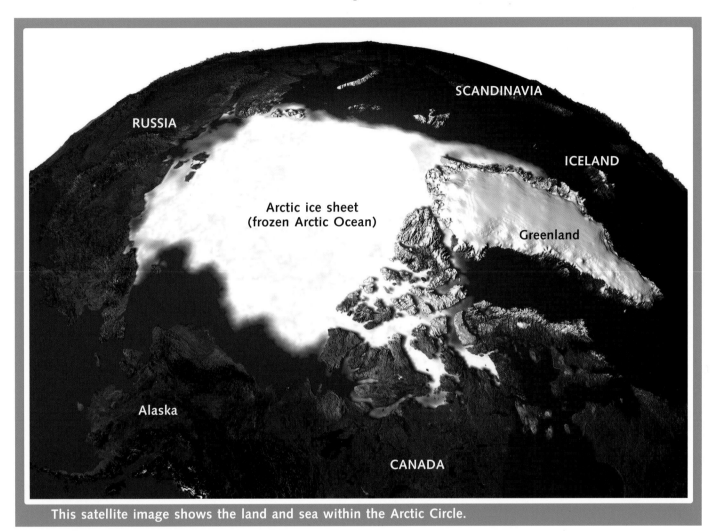

SCANDINAVIA

RUSSIA

ICELAND

Arctic ice sheet
(frozen Arctic Ocean)

Greenland

Alaska

CANADA

This satellite image shows the land and sea within the Arctic Circle.

Arctic Ocean

The Arctic Ocean is Earth's smallest ocean. Some of it is permanently covered in ice.

The North Pole is not an area of land but part of the frozen Arctic Ocean. This **ice sheet** partly melts during the warmer summer months and freezes again in the winter.

Greenland

Greenland, the world's largest island, is covered by an **ice cap** more than 1.2 miles (2 kilometers) thick. This ice cap contains one-eighth of Earth's ice mass. It is made of snow that has fallen on Greenland and built up over thousands of years. When the ice cap melts it produces fresh water.

Fact ZONE
The Arctic ice sheet has an average thickness of 9.8 feet (3 meters). Nuclear-powered submarines travel beneath it.

Global Warming and Greenhouse Gases

Global warming is caused by the **greenhouse effect**. **Greenhouse gases** trap the heat from the sun in Earth's **atmosphere**. This heat leads to an increase in Earth's surface temperature.

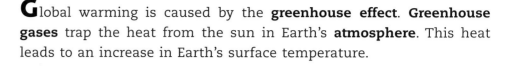

Greenhouse Gases

Greenhouse gases occur naturally in Earth's atmosphere, but human activities contribute to these gases. These human activities are increasing as the world's population increases.

Scientists now agree that in recent decades the amount of greenhouse gases in the atmosphere has increased. More of the sun's heat is being trapped, leading to further global warming. The term "global warming" in this book refers to the effects of this extra heat being trapped.

The Impact of Human Activities

Human activities generate three main greenhouse gases: **carbon dioxide**, **methane**, and **nitrous oxide**. Carbon dioxide is produced when **fossil fuels** such as coal and oil are burned. The level of carbon dioxide in the air is also affected by the clearing of forests, as trees and other plants absorb carbon dioxide to produce oxygen, which is vital to life on Earth. Methane is produced naturally by livestock such as cows and sheep who release it as part of their digestive process. It is also produced when substances such as manure and waste products in landfills begin to ferment, or turn sour. Nitrous oxide is produced when certain fertilizers are used to grow crops.

The greenhouse effect is the trapping of the Sun's heat because of certain gases in the atmosphere.

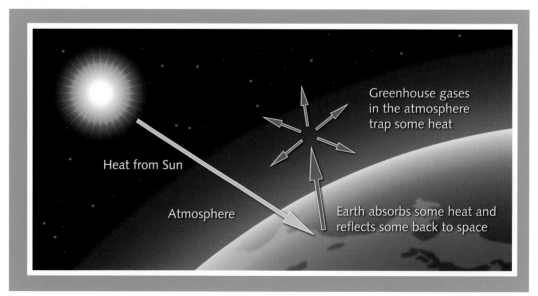

Greenhouse gases in the atmosphere trap some heat

Heat from Sun

Atmosphere

Earth absorbs some heat and reflects some back to space

Possible Effects of Global Warming

Scientists are making predictions about the effects of global warming. Global warming could affect the environment and humans in many different ways.

Fact ZONE
Rising temperatures have caused most of Earth's mass **extinction** events in the past.

POSSIBLE EFFECTS OF GLOBAL WARMING IN THE ARCTIC

POSSIBLE EVENT	PREDICTED RESULT	IMPACT ON THE ARCTIC
MELTING OF ICE CAP AND ICE SHEETS	✳ Rising global sea levels ✳ Loss of **habitat** for native wildlife	✳ Disturbance of hunting and traditional way of life for **indigenous** peoples ✳ Endangerment of polar bear
THAWING OF **PERMAFROST**	✳ Decomposition of the soil	✳ Disruption to transportation routes and construction ✳ More carbon dioxide and methane released
LONGER, WARMER MONTHS	✳ Lengthening of the growing season in some places	✳ New land for farming in Greenland ✳ Ability to grow new crops
MORE WINTER SNOW	✳ Less **lichen** and moss	✳ Lower caribou numbers due to lack of food ✳ Loss of traditional hunting for indigenous peoples
MELTING OF SUMMER SEA ICE	✳ Opening of Northwest Passage	✳ New and quicker sea route ✳ Improved economy due to greater tourism and trade ✳ Disagreement over passage ownership

Climate Change in the Arctic

The effects of climate change are more visible in the Arctic because ice is quickly affected by even small temperature changes.

Average temperatures in the Arctic are rising much faster than they are in other regions of Earth. Scientists have predicted that a global temperature increase of 35.6°F (2°C) would be a 32.9°F (0.5°C) increase at the **equator** but a 41–42.8°F (5–6°C) increase at the North Pole.

Melting Ice Sheet

The polar ice sheet, the permanent ice covering the Arctic Ocean, is shrinking. If this continues, parts of the Arctic Ocean will be ice-free during the summer months by the end of this century.

The melting of ice that was once permanent is already affecting the Arctic's indigenous peoples and wildlife. Some species are changing their feeding and **migration** patterns, making it more difficult for people to hunt them.

Melting ice will also cause global temperatures to increase further. Land and water do not reflect heat away from Earth as well as snow and ice do.

This satellite image shows the average minimum area of Arctic sea ice in 1979–1981.

Melting Glaciers and Ice Caps

The melting of glaciers and ice caps also contributes to rising sea levels. Recent satellite images show that the rate of melting of the Greenland ice cap is a cause for concern. Scientists are predicting a 20-inch (50-centimeter) rise in global sea levels by 2100 due to melting ice caps. If the Greenland ice cap were to melt completely, global sea levels would rise by 20 feet (6 meters).

More Precipitation

As Earth's surface temperature increases there is likely to be more **precipitation**. Using climate models, some scientists predict an increase of between 30 percent and 50 percent in the Arctic. The precipitation would fall mostly as snow, but some would fall as rain as temperatures rise.

This satellite image shows the average minimum area of Arctic sea ice in 2003–2005.

The Natural World of the Arctic

The Arctic is one of the harshest environments on Earth. It has cold winters, where temperatures drop to –29°F (–34°C). Summers are short and cool, averaging 41°F (5°C), although temperatures can rise to 59°F (15°C). On average, less than 20 inches (50 cm) of precipitation falls each year, mainly as snow. During the winter there is no daylight for three months at the North Pole.

Arctic Ecosystems

There are three Arctic **ecosystems**:

- the Arctic Ocean, which supports major fisheries, including cod

- ice sheets, which provide shelter and hunting grounds for polar bears, seals, and walruses

- flat land areas called tundra, where grasses, mosses, and lichen grow, providing food for caribou, musk ox, and arctic hare. Trees do not grow here because it is too cold, the ground is frozen, and during the winter there is not enough light.

Grasses of the tundra are a food source for Arctic animals in the region.

Arctic Wildlife

Arctic animals have thick coats to keep them warm. Seals and whales living in the icy waters have blubber, a thick layer of fat beneath their skin. Some of the world's most distinctive mammals live in the Arctic, including the polar bear, musk ox, and caribou. Smaller animals include the lemming, arctic hare, arctic fox, and the wolf. Bird life is abundant in summer, with millions of migratory birds visiting to breed.

Fragile Ecosystems

The Arctic supports some unique ecosystems that are sensitive to changes in the region's climate. Arctic animals have adapted to extremely low temperatures, and limited sunlight and precipitation. They have also adapted to a short growing season. Due to low temperatures, vegetation only grows for a limited period of fifty to one hundred days a year. It is too cold for vegetation to grow at any other time. Changes to the climate could dramatically alter the **food chain** and ecosystem of the Arctic.

Arctic Food Chain

Sea ice, which is frozen seawater, plays an important role in the Arctic food chain. It is a source of food for krill, which feed on the algae that grow on the underside of the sea ice. Krill, in turn, are eaten by fish. Fewer algae and krill would lower the number of fish, impacting whales, walruses, seals, and polar bears, that feed on the fish.

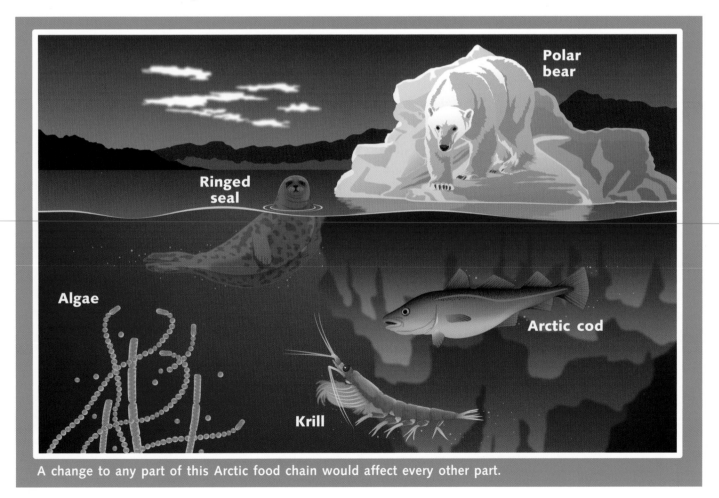

A change to any part of this Arctic food chain would affect every other part.

Polar Bears

Background

Length	up to 9.8 feet (3 meters)
Weight	male: up to 1,500 pounds (680 kilograms), female: up to 551 lb (250 kg)
Main food	ringed seals

Polar bears are found in the Arctic regions of Alaska, Canada, Greenland, Norway, and Russia. They number between 20,000 and 25,000.

Polar bears can survive temperatures of up to –49°F (–45°C). They are also known as great white bears or nunak.

The polar bear has been listed as an endangered species by the United States Secretary of the Interior. It could become the first mammal to lose its habitat due to climate change. There are also fears that the bear could become extinct within the next one hundred years.

Fact ZONE

The white fur of a polar bear provides camouflage as it sneaks up on seals. If a bear sees a seal's breathing hole, it waits by the hole and drags the seal out as soon as its head appears.

This polar bear is waiting for a seal to emerge from beneath the surface.

Melting Ice Sheets

Each summer the Arctic ice sheet melts at an increasing rate. The sea ice in Hudson Bay, Canada, which is partly within the Arctic Circle, has been melting up to three weeks earlier than it did in the 1970s. As the ice sheet **retreats** northward the habitat of the polar bear shrinks. Polar bears spend their time raising their young on the ice sheets and hunting seals to feed them. As the ice sheets melt and break up, bears are forced to swim longer distances to find food. Although the bears are good swimmers, some become exhausted and drown before reaching the next ice sheet.

Disappearing Food Sources

Unable to find food in the water, polar bears are forced to hunt on land for alternative sources of food, such as caribou. However, polar bears are slow runners and no match for the fast caribou. Furthermore, caribou meat alone does not provide polar bears with enough fat in their diet to survive the winter months. As a result polar bears become thin. Thin female polar bears are unable to feed their cubs as they do not make enough high-fat milk. They are also unable to survive on the lower stores of fat on them during the winter months.

Polar bears, such as this one in Alaska, venture into towns when their natural food source is less available.

The impact of climate change on...

Caribou

Background

Height   up to 5 ft (1.5 m) at the shoulder

Weight   up to 701 lb (318 kg)

Caribou (known as reindeer in Europe) are the most common large land mammals in the Arctic.

They gather in herds of up to 100,000 in the summer for the calving season, feeding on small shrubs across the vast tundra. In the winter the herds scatter in search of moss and lichen.

Caribou are an important part of the culture of the indigenous Inuit people. As hunters, the Inuit not only use the caribou as a source of food, but also to make warm clothing and tents.

Fact ZONE

A baby caribou is able to stand and walk an hour after it is born. It can run when it is a day old.

Caribou numbers appear to be decreasing. Researchers studying the Porcupine River herd in Alaska have seen a steady decline from 187,000 in 1989 to 120,000 in 2007.

Caribou travel in large herds during the Arctic summer.

More Snow in Winter

In winter more snow is falling, which makes it harder for the caribou to reach moss and lichen. As a result, many caribou have reduced body fat, and calf survival rates are lower. Deeper snow also makes running from predators more difficult.

Food Shortages in Summer

Warmer weather also causes grass and plants to become green earlier. This is a bonus during calving season, but the grass and plants become scarce by early summer. This means the caribou may not be able to get sufficient amounts of food to enable them to fatten up for the winter, when food is in short supply.

More Mosquitoes

In recent years swarms of mosquitoes have increased because the warmer weather has given them a longer breeding season. The mosquitoes torment the caribou and reduce their ability to feed. Caribou give birth each year, but in a poor feeding season they would not have sufficient fat reserves to see them through the winter. As a result, they may not have calves. Those caribou that do get pregnant with low fat reserves are likely to produce weaker calves. This means the death rate among mothers and calves will be higher.

Fact ZONE
A mosquito can suck a tablespoon of blood a day from a caribou.

Caribou sometimes take to water to escape mosquitoes.

Permafrost

Background

Permafrost is a layer of soil that remains permanently frozen. It covers 20 percent of the Earth's land area but is mostly found in the Arctic and Antarctic regions.

Global warming has caused areas of permafrost to thaw. The thawing of the frozen ground causes a number of problems.

Damage and Collapse

Soggy soil cannot support structures built on it. This results in the collapse of houses and other buildings. Roads and train tracks may buckle and twist as the ground thaws, drainpipes may crack.

Fact ZONE

In areas where the permafrost has thawed, the roots of some trees can no longer hold onto the soil. Some groups of trees lean in many different directions, and have been called "drunken trees."

Thawing permafrost has caused the soil beneath this house to move, damaging the gutter along the roof.

Methane Release

In Siberia an area the size of France and Germany, about 386,102 square miles (one million square kilometers) has started to thaw for the first time since the most recent Ice Age. It is the world's largest frozen peat bog. There are fears that if it thaws completely it will release billions of tons of methane into the atmosphere. Methane absorbs heat 20 times more effectively than carbon dioxide. This would add to global warming.

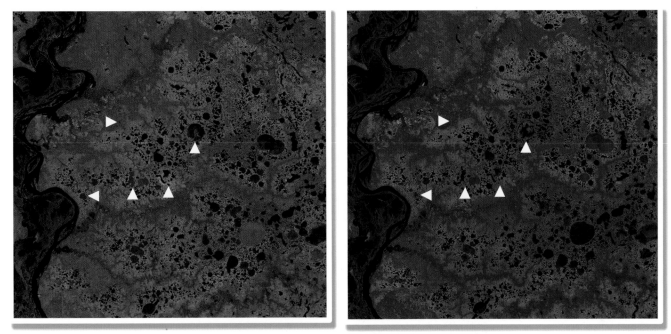

These satellite images show Siberian lakes in 1973 (left) and 2002 (right). Arrows point to the lakes that have shrunk significantly. The melting permafrost has caused the lake water to drain deeper into the ground.

CASE STUDY

Alaskan Permafrost

Computer models show that about 10 feet (3 meters) of permafrost could melt in Alaska by 2100. This would change large areas of forest and tundra into swamps. Swamps contain vast amounts of methane. The methane has been trapped in the frozen soil. If the soil thaws, the methane would be released into the atmosphere, increasing the levels of greenhouse gases that are contributing to global warming.

Greenland's Ice Cap

Background

Greenland is the world's largest island and its capital city is Nuuk.

Most of the island is covered in thick ice known as the Greenland ice cap. This ice is 4,921 ft (1,500 m) thick on average but can be up to 14,108 ft (4,300 m) thick.

The ice cap is so heavy that the land below it has been pressed down into the shape of a bowl. It contains about 10 percent of Earth's fresh water.

Greenland has a population of only 57,000 who live in the towns and settlements along the ice-free sections of the coast. Greenlanders make their living from fishing.

Global warming poses serious problems for Greenland's ice cap. Climate experts believe that an increase in temperature of only 5.4°F (3°C) would begin to melt it. If this happens a time will come when the ice cap begins to break up.

Fact ZONE

An island covered in ice and called Greenland sounds unusual. Eric the Red, a Viking, is believed to have discovered the island in 982 CE. He named it Greenland, hoping to encourage settlers from Norway to move there.

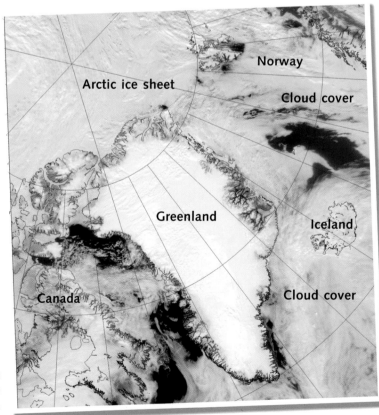

This satellite image shows the ice cap that covers almost all of Greenland.

Melting Ice Cap

Some scientists report that the predicted increase in temperature of 14.4°F (8°C) by the year 2350 will make Greenland's ice cap melt completely within 1,000 years. If this happens, sea levels around the world will increase by 20–23 ft (6–7 m). This would flood most of the world's major coastal cities and low-lying countries.

During the summer, surface melt on the ice cap is occurring. This results in water running through cracks in the ice to the base of the ice cap. This helps the ice flow faster to the coast. Recent scientific evidence shows the ice to be melting three times faster than it was five years ago.

This meltwater is flowing from the base of a glacier in Norway.

Humans in the Arctic

About 13 million people live in the Arctic. Four million are indigenous peoples who have lived in the region for more than 10,000 years. Indigenous people survive on the resources of the land and the sea and prosper under some of the harshest conditions on Earth.

People of the Arctic live in settlements that vary from small, traditional communities to industrialized cities. The Arctic has limited employment opportunities. Many people hope that the growing tourist industry and development of gas reserves and mining will improve their lives.

Children living in the Arctic can do many things in the winter, including skiing, skating, ice hockey and playing in the snow. In the summer there are 20 hours of daylight and the sky is never totally dark.

The Arctic weather is so cold that water must be trucked into the communities, and sewage is also taken away by truck. Air travel is often the only way to reach some of the northern communities. Many people have snowmobiles but dogsleds are still used by one group of indigenous peoples, the Inuit.

Isolated Arctic towns, such as Ilulissat in Greenland, have limited business opportunities.

The Indigenous Peoples of the Arctic

The Inuit ("the people") are the largest group of indigenous peoples in the Canadian Arctic. Other indigenous groups live in the Arctic, too.

INDIGENOUS PEOPLES OF THE ARCTIC

LOCATION	INDIGENOUS PEOPLE
ALASKA, CANADA, GREENLAND	Inuit
NORTHERN SCANDINAVIA	Saami
SIBERIA	Chukchi and Nenet

Inuit were once called Eskimo, which means "eaters of raw meat." Most Inuit live in the Canadian province of Nunavut ("our land"), where they govern themselves. Despite many recent changes, indigenous culture remains strong and communities are still closely linked to native wildlife and local resources.

To dress warmly the Inuit wear long coats that reach down to their knees. Clothing, food, and other essentials can be bought from a store. Traditional clothing of boots, pants, and coats made from caribou skins are still used.

Although their homes are modern, the Inuit still build igloos in the winter and use tents in the summer when they go hunting.

Fact ZONE
The Inuit have 20 different words for types of snow.

Some houses in the Arctic are built on stilts for stability.

The Inuit and Other Indigenous Peoples

Background

The Inuit are the indigenous inhabitants of the North American Arctic. They live in Canada, Alaska, and Greenland and have close relatives in Russia.

They pride themselves on being great hunters. Traditionally, caribou and seal were the most important animals, providing food and skin for clothing, blankets, tents, and boats. Oil from seal blubber was used for cooking and lamps. Bones, ivory, and wood were used to make tools.

Since the 1940s, there has been more contact between the Inuit and the outside world. With better medical care, the population grew larger and could not sustain itself by hunting only. Many Inuit have moved to permanent settlements where they can access food, jobs, and education. The Inuit were considered one of the healthiest people on Earth before such changes in diet and lifestyle took hold.

Global warming has made traditional hunting and fishing more difficult for the Inuit. The melting permafrost has damaged buildings and affected transportation. Similar problems are being faced by indigenous groups in other Arctic regions.

Fact ZONE

Because of warmer temperatures, the children of Pangnirtung on Baffin Island have taken up golf during the dry dusty summers. Elders contrast this with pictures of villagers clad in furs from previous summer months of years ago.

The Arctic has experienced warmer summers in recent years, so more outdoor activities are possible.

Hunting for Food

With warmer temperatures the seasonal migrations of the large herds of caribou have become more difficult to predict. Fish and wildlife are following the retreating ice caps northward, forcing the Inuit to travel further on their hunting trips.

Melting Permafrost

Melting permafrost is also creating problems. Roads are being damaged and airport runways and harbor supports are collapsing due to the softening soil. The small settlement of Shismaref in Alaska has been forced to move inland. Rising lea levels and melting permafrost have caused **erosion** of the narrow piece of land where houses were located.

These indigenous people are hunting for crab and fish.

CASE STUDY

Mackenzie River Basin, Canada

The Canadian government has been studying the Mackenzie River Basin in northwestern Canada, which lies partly within the Arctic Circle. This area is heating up faster than any place on Earth. The warm temperatures there sparked widespread wildfires in 1995. The fires forced the evacuation of the small community of Tulita, inhabited mostly by indigenous people. The wildlife has been very important to the local community and will probably not return to the area for many years because of the fires.

The Northwest Passage

Background

The Northwest Passage is a sea route through the Arctic Ocean. It leads ships along the coast of Greenland, up to Baffin Bay and through the Canadian Arctic Archipelago to the Beaufort Sea. From there the passage enters the Bering Strait, which lies between the U.S. state of Alaska and the Russian Federation. Between the 1400s and 1900s, many explorers tried to complete this journey in order to find a new sea route between Europe and Asia. It was Roald Amundsen who first navigated the Northwest Passage successfully between 1903 and 1906.

Since Amundsen's journey, the Northwest Passage has not been viable as a commercial shipping channel due to the amount of sea ice in the region. However, global warming has reduced the amount of sea ice in recent years. Satellite photos taken in 2007 show the Northwest Passage to be ice-free for the first time. Within forty years, ships may be using this new sea route regularly. The Northwest Passage could reduce the voyage from Europe to Asia by as much as 4,971 miles (8,000 km).

Fact ZONE

The Northwest Passage would not be accessible all year round and would require ice-strengthened vessels.

This satellite image, taken in August 2007, shows a section of the Northwest Passage, with large ice-free sections visible. The red line marks one of several possible shipping routes through the area.

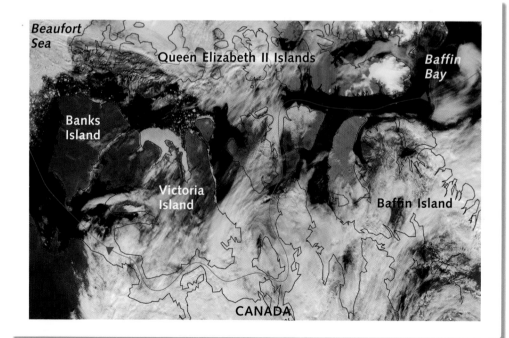

Opening the Arctic Frontier

A new shipping route would open up isolated areas of northern Canada and Alaska. This would have a huge impact on the local small communities. Increased trade, navigation, and shipping services would bring greater wealth to the region. Adventure tours and cruise ships would have new routes to explore.

The melting also means the possibility of undersea gas and oil exploration in the Arctic. The United States Geological Survey, an organization that studies the geology of the United States, estimates that the Arctic has as much as 25 percent of the world's undiscovered oil and gas.

Ownership of the Northwest Passage

Access to this new area may be a problem. Canada has already claimed ownership over parts of the Northwest Passage. It wants to control the area and decide who can use it. Other countries argue that it should be international, allowing all vessels to travel through it.

Access to the Northwest Passage route would allow more ships to visit the Arctic region.

The impact of climate change on...

Farming

Background

Cold weather in the Arctic has, until recently, meant limited farming activity. In the past, the land could only be used for growing potatoes and herding sheep and reindeer.

One of the benefits of climate change is taking place in Greenland. The warmer temperatures are creating many opportunities for farming.

Fact ZONE

Due to lengthy transportation times from other countries, imported fruit and vegetables used to be of poor quality in Greenland. Now, warmer temperatures have allowed farmers to grow some of these fruit and vegetables themselves, ensuring fresh produce.

The changing climate in Greenland has opened up more land for farming.

Farming Boom

Today's warmer conditions and longer growing seasons are allowing new crops such as broccoli and cabbage to be grown in Greenland. Cattle are also being kept and for the first time fresh milk is available.

This new farming is limited to the southern coastal areas. In Qaqortoq the average temperature has increased by 2.3°F (1.3°C) over the past 30 years. This has added two weeks to the growing season. A 120-day growing season combined with up to 20 hours of daylight in the summer means that more and different types of food can be grown.

These ranchers in Greenland have benefited from the warmer conditions, which provide them with more grazing land for cattle.

CASE STUDY

A Farming Pioneer

Sofus Frederiksen is one of Greenland's new farming pioneers. He owns 9 of the 19 cows on the island. In summer they graze the slopes, feeding on grass and rye. Frederiksen also has to harvest enough hay and rye in the summer to feed his cattle in the winter months. He has been building a small **hydroelectric** facility on his farm to warm the barns where the cattle live in winter.

Taking Action on Climate Change

Changes in climate are providing strong evidence of global warming. The international community is working to understand and act on its impact.

Human activity is generally accepted as the main cause of global warming and climate change. Decreasing the amount of carbon dioxide and other greenhouse gases in the atmosphere is the best way to slow global warming.

Global Response

A total of 170 countries have signed the **Kyoto Protocol**. Industrialized, developed countries agreed to cut their combined greenhouse gas emissions to 5 percent below their 1990 level by 2012.

At the **United Nations** Climate Change Conference in Bali in 2007 delegates agreed to discuss a new climate change agreement to replace the Kyoto Protocol, which expires in 2012. These objectives were discussed further at the United Nations Framework Convention on Climate Change in Poznan, Poland, in December 2008. The purpose of the discussions was to set targets for future greenhouse gas reductions. Many scientists suggest cuts of 60 percent are needed to avoid the worst consequences of global warming.

Fact ZONE

The United States, which has not signed the Kyoto Protocol, produces 20 percent of all greenhouse gases. Some people believe the Kyoto Protocol will have little effect.

CASE STUDY

The Kyoto Protocol

The Kyoto Protocol is an agreement between certain countries that sets targets to reduce greenhouse gas emissions. It was negotiated in Kyoto, Japan, in 1997.

Each country that has signed the Kyoto Protocol has agreed to its own particular target.

The United States is the only developed country that hasn't signed the agreement.

Countries such as China and India do not have to meet the emission targets because they have only recently begun to develop their industries. Other industrial countries have caused the current levels of greenhouse gases in the atmosphere to rise.

The Kyoto Protocol will be replaced by a new climate change agreement in 2012.

Arctic Response: Renewable Energy

Arctic communities use a lot of energy per person because of the cold weather. The Arctic Energy Alliance of Canada is promoting the use of **renewable energy**. Small hydroelectric facilities, wind turbines, solar energy, and use of **biofuels** are encouraged. There is also a focus on energy efficiency. Projects are designed to improve the efficiency of diesel power generation, which most of the communities rely on.

This hydroelectric power plant in Lapland in northern Finland uses the energy of water to generate power.

The Inuit Circumpolar Council (ICC) aims to bring the Arctic and Inuit perspectives on climate change to the attention of decision makers. Members have delivered speeches worldwide, including to the U.S. Senate. The ICC protects the interests of all indigenous peoples in the Arctic.

The Inuit Circumpolar Council took part in the United Nations Climate Change Conference in Bali in 2007.

29

The Future

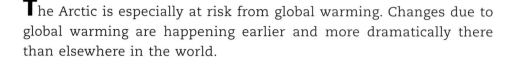

The Arctic is especially at risk from global warming. Changes due to global warming are happening earlier and more dramatically there than elsewhere in the world.

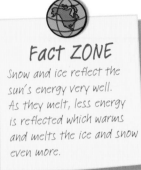

Bad News and Good News

Arctic ice is melting rapidly and could cause sea levels to rise. The natural environments of animals such as the polar bear and caribou are threatened. The indigenous peoples of the Arctic are being forced to change their hunting and fishing culture. Frozen soils are thawing, causing housing and transportation problems.

Some farmers and shipping companies may benefit from a warmer Arctic. A warmer Arctic would be more tourist-friendly, meaning more jobs in tourism may be created. Development of coal and oil fields previously hidden beneath the ice may bring money to the region.

There is evidence that global warming is already affecting the Arctic. What happens in the future may depend on what humans do about further global warming.

The indigenous way of life in the Arctic is changing because of global warming.

Glossary

atmosphere	the layer of gases that surrounds Earth
biofuel	a renewable fuel made from plant material such as corn
carbon dioxide	a greenhouse gas produced by burning fossil fuels and clearing forests
carbon footprint	a measure of the carbon dioxide humans produce while doing their activities
climate change	changes in weather patterns caused by global warming
ecosystem	a group of living things and their habitat
equator	an imaginary line that circles Earth and lies exactly halfway between the North and South poles
erosion	the wearing away of land by wind, water, and ice
extinction	the death of every member of a group of living things
food chain	an ordered linkage of living things. Living things higher in the order eat the living things below them in the chain
fossil fuel	a fuel such as coal or oil made of fossilized remains of plants
glaciers	slow-moving frozen rivers of ice
global warming	an increase in the average surface temperature of Earth
greenhouse effect	the warming of Earth's surface due to trapping of heat in the atmosphere
greenhouse gas	a gas that helps trap the sun's heat in the atmosphere
habitat	the surroundings in which an animal or plant lives
hydroelectric	generating electricity by the power of running water
Ice Age	a period when temperatures were lower and large areas of Earth were ice-covered
ice cap	an ice-covered area of land
ice sheet	a large body of floating ice
indigenous	native to an area
Kyoto Protocol	a special guideline that was created with the aim of reducing greenhouse gases
lichen	a small flat plant made of a fungus and algae growing together
methane	a greenhouse gas produced by cattle and rotting plant material
migration	movement from one place to another
nitrous oxide	a greenhouse gas produced from fertilizers
permafrost	ground that is always frozen
precipitation	rain, snow, hail, and sleet
renewable energy	energy from virtually unlimited sources, such as the sun
retreat	move backward
United Nations	a group of countries that have agreed to work together on matters such as peace, security, and cooperation

Index